My Life with Geeks and Freaks

Claudia Christian

Yard Dog Press
710 W. Redbud Lane
Alma, AR 72921-7247

http://www.yarddogpress.com

Edited by Selina Rosen
Copy Editor Leonard R. Bishop
Technical Editor Lynn Stranathan
Cover photography by Robert Zuckerman
Graphic artist Gilles Nuytens
Cover design by Holly Evans

ISBN: 1-893687-85-6
ISBN-13: 918-1-893687-85-1

Copyright © 2007 by Claudia Christian

First Edition June 1, 2007
Printed in the United States of America
0 9 8 7 6 5 4 3 2 1

This book is dedicated to my trusted
web mistress-accountant-shlepper-sherpa guide-booker-tax
woman-cheerleader and friend; Miss Holly (20/20) Evans.
If it wasn't for you kid,
I never could have become a Holiday Inn Gold member!
In all seriousness, here's to our higher aspirations coming
true very soon.... Double C

A BRIEF HERSTORY

I have always loved people stories. The one about the little boy forced to eat out of a dog bowl that goes on to make a fortune writing about having to eat out of a dog bowl. The one about the poor Irish boy who dreams about eating an egg who goes on to make millions writing about dreaming about eating an egg. I have never eaten out of a dog bowl, and I rarely dream about eating an egg.

That doesn't mean I don't have any stories to tell.

It was 10:30 PM, March 23rd, 2007, and I was standing in the cold, wet cluster fuck that is JFK, waiting for someone to pick me up. The driver was either stuck in traffic or just waiting to see if I would actually implode; I'm not sure which. He finally got there and took me to a Holiday Inn where I quickly dumped my stuff and then got back in the car where I sat for 40 minutes while listening to bad music and geek chatter. I then had to be funny, amusing, and utterly charming at midnight, on live radio.

I had been traveling since 8:00 AM that morning, and I was not being paid to do this. So why was I doing it? Because, apparently, I am not sane. The plane had been delayed nearly two hours on the ground at Burbank airport. We had then slowly pulled into JFK over the course of an hour after a turbulent six hours in the air, and then I was standing in the freezing rain for an hour, waiting for that moron to come get me. I could have been in Paris by then, sipping a café au lait on the Rue St. Germaine.

And did I mention I wasn't getting paid for this?

I spent an hour or more on the radio show with some lovely people including one jolly fellow named Adam, who had written a song for me titled "muse of the geeks." I think that's a title

I will use for the rest of my life.

I then went back to my hotel room where I unpacked my few clothes and cosmetics in a room that reeked of cigarettes. I was staying in the non-smoking room I had requested. Unfortunately it happened to be right next to a room holding a dozen nicotine junkies who obviously took great pleasure in blowing their smoke though the vents so that it traveled directly into my room. It smelled like the bottom of an ashtray, but I washed my face and lit a few candles – I always bring some with me for pungent rooms – then I lay down to read a book.

In the old days I would have raided the mini-bar or have gone downstairs and had a few glasses of wine before trying to sleep. Now that I don't drink, I was stone cold sober as I lay on the bed trying to read and wondering just what the hell I was doing in a Holiday Inn in Stony Brook, New York on a Friday night.

I got to ask myself basically that same question over and over again as I spent most of the next 48 hours sitting in a gymnasium at the University of Stony Brook, signing a few photos and doing talk after talk to hung-over, exhausted, brain-dead audiences who barely laughed at my jokes.

I once again endured people asking me why they had not seen me on TV lately. I forced a smile and answered. "I live in London. You can see me on TV there."

As always there were the people who have no idea who I am but took great pleasure in standing in front of my table and handling every single one of my photos with their greasy hands before asking for one and then being appalled that we are charging for them.

I worked nearly 16 hours on Saturday doing everything from signing things to question and answer panels, improv shows, judging costume contests, posing for photos, and then doing more panels which had topics but usually turned into Q and A's. As usual I didn't take a meal break but just inhaled some peanut M and M's and a diet coke at my table instead. After paying commission, cost of photos, shipping etc, I made less than minimum wage for the weekend.

I feared for my sanity; I considered going to India to "find myself." I sat on the plane home trying to justify the whole trip. I thought… "At least the fans had a good time, they like me… they really, really like me!" Then the other part of my brain yells out, "Shut up Sally!"

I lay back in my jet blue seat and started to look at my life through a mental microscope for the next six and a half hours. It wasn't the first time, nor I am sure will it be the last, that I will consider the whole of my existence with my ass forced into an uncomfortable airline seat.

After all, this is my life.

Glendale, California, August 10th 1965

I happen to have been delivered into the world during one of the worst race riots in history. If I was cognitive, I'm sure I could tell you interesting anecdotes; however, I was just a pigeon-toed – though much anticipated after three boys – infant girl.

My mother had been sure I was going to be deformed or an alien because apparently I "felt different" when she was carrying me. A fairly large leap of her imagination I think, to go from "gee this pregnancy feels a little different" to "get it out of me; it's clearly a freak!" which is apparently what she yelled at my father before my birth. It should come as no surprise then that I went into drama as a profession.

Now remember, I was born right in the middle of a huge race riot, but my black nanny took one look at my turned-in feet and decided that she was going to heal me instead of quitting her job and storming out to march. God bless her, she kept me from having to wear metal braces for my formative years. She massaged my little feet every night and made me sleep with a towel between them, forcing them out, and lo and behold, I am not pigeon toed. I do, however, have ugly feet.

I know that we lived in Glendale for a while and that my Dad worked for Shell Oil Company. Shell likes to transfer their people a lot, no doubt because they are evil and enjoy ruining kid's lives by yanking them out of school just as they start to make friends.

We wound up in Westport Connecticut, and things were great. My three older brothers, Patrick, Jimmy, and Vincent and I would build snow forts. They made me a dollhouse for my fourth Christmas, and I thoroughly enjoyed it. I also had my own outdoor playhouse which came in handy to get away from my brothers when they weren't being so nice.

I had a bizarre ringing in my ears at that age, so I did what any sensible four year old would do. I'd go to my playhouse and pretend it was a phone ringing. I'd answer it, and it would be from the animal kingdom, just one of my animal friends on the other end wanting to shoot the shit with me for awhile. I would walk around with my fingers made into a phone pressed up to my ear and chat until the ringing went away.

No wonder they built me my own little mad house outside...far away from the main house... and the neighbors. Bellevue for the under five crowd! The tinnitus eventually went away, so I developed a new unattractive habit – a spastic blinking eye thing that I first did to cover the fact that I was crying during Walt Disney's *Wonderful World of Disney* screening of *Sleeping Beauty*. There I sat minding my own business, caught up in the sorrow and glamour of Sleeping Beauty looking so good on that death slab, the prince just about to kiss her, hot fat tears running down my cherubic cheeks, when all of a sudden a cackle from the bowels of hell scratched my fantasy record to a screeching halt!

My brothers, little shits that they were, were pissing themselves with glee at the sight of my tear-soaked face, so I yelled with all the conviction I could muster that I was not crying, I had something in my eye! I then proceeded to "pretend" to get it out by blinking and stretching my face into a gnome-like contortion; I'm sure I looked like one of those dried-apple doll heads they sell in "whimsical" tourist shops in the Midwest. Places with names like "Butterballs and Moonbeams" or "Apple Jack's Hideaway."

I pretended I had something in my eye for two solid embarrassing years until magically the facial contorting simply went away. My mother, bless her, rarely mentioned it.

The true excitement of life comes from experiencing something for the first time. The absolute bliss that comes from absorbing yourself completely in the newness of an event is something that I recall with great clarity. The first teacher I liked, the aching vividness of my first love at twelve years old.

I spent an entire summer of my life on a flag pole because whilst sliding down I discovered the joy of instant orgasms! I thought I was being sneaky and subtle, but apparently my Popeye sized forearms from climbing up the pole a hundred times a day and my sudden obsession with the great outdoors even when it was pissing down rain, did not go unnoticed by my family. I am still teased about it to this day.

Things are always brilliantly fresh when they're new. That old cliché of the first taste of ice cream is heartbreakingly true for me. Things are just old now, and I can count on one hand the times I can recall in recent memory that I have been truly happy, or laughing for real; not some forced "God, I really want to be having a good time" laugh.

I suppose that freshness, those good "first time" experiences make up for all of the other appalling things that happen to you as a child. The accidents, the broken bones that rape your summer plans, school chums who betray you, teachers and parents who let you down, and boys who never look your way. Those first-time injustices and pains are also felt surprisingly fresh and viscerally as if to temper the good feelings in a conservative Victorian "can't enjoy life too much!" sort of way.

I recall my father always telling me to watch my back after something wonderful would happen to me, as if you had to even out the good with something horrid right around the corner. Years later in a rather sterile hypnotist's office in Encino, California, I came upon the realization that my inhuman number of car accidents always occurred after something good happened to me. A job, a new man, a fun trip... were always followed by a horrific accident which would claim my attention and my life for the next few months as I recovered physically and financially, not to mention the court dates, lost driving privileges and other nuisances. Thanks Dad!

My three brothers fell into fairly neat packages. Patrick, old enough to be the care giver in some capacity, and therefore less likely to feel the need to beat me up, Jimmy, too busy with other things to really notice me, and Vincent, my youngest brother, whose life eventually became one serious effort to rid the planet of my presence. It's funny how he cannot recall his puberty-fuelled rages against me, hard to believe this genetic engineer with a PhD in physics can't muster up the brain power to re-member the dreaded "grandpa's cane" exercises or the old "snot spittle in Claude's face" routines we used to *so* enjoy. I exacted a modicum of revenge years later at the wise old age of ten when I would bellydance for his friends for a nickel a dance; I bought a hell of a lot of candy that summer.

We lived in Westport, Connecticut, and I was three the first time my mom let the boys walk me to the corner store, a place called "Christies." I walked to the corner with the troglodytes I knew as my brothers. They ran across the street and left me standing on the corner alone – no doubt because they thought it was funny.

I knew not to cross the street alone, but I hadn't been taught the "don't bend over into a stranger's car" rule, so when a car with a man pulled up and asked me if I wanted to touch his "frog" which he was vigorously pulling at in his lap, I almost got in for a closer look. Thank God my oldest brother Patrick ran back across to get me, or I could have ended up a sick statis-tic.

My first friendship left a rather indelible mark on me. When I was three Jill Freeman was my best friend in the universe, really my only friend. It was through my friendship with her that I first grasped the concept of "mine." She was "My" friend not my brothers', not my parents', but all mine. And I will freely admit I was a little possessive.

You have to remember I had three older brothers; I had no privacy except for the moments that my mother provided by ushering the boys out and away and telling them, "Leave your sister alone!" Then I would have the blessed peace that I so craved even then. Solitude has always been a must for me. Ironi-cally it's biting me on the ass now at 40, and for the first time in my life I have felt pangs of loneliness at times. These were especially strong when I first moved country to London almost three years ago. As they say, be careful what you wish for...

When I was five years old my father was transferred to Houston Texas, land of the big hair! And big cars and big steaks! And all that crap. All I saw was a disgusting cement cesspool, and all I heard were revolting twangy accents I could barely understand.

Why did everyone act like they just got off a horse? A lot of big sniffs in through the nose and pulling up of pants like Barney did on the *Andy Griffith Show*. I didn't like Houston. I can remember that it was dark in the mornings when we waited for the bus, and the crawdads would be crawling all over the gutters. It was humid, and the only place to swim was a bayou with poisonous water moccasins in it. Oh, and they hated "foreigners," so with a German mom and East Coast accents, we were practically foreign exchange students to them.

My definitive moment came during the Pumpkin Circle around Halloween, a very Americanized tradition of sucking money out of people and filling kids with candy and dentist's pockets with cash. We were all sitting around this little circle doing some lame game where you have to keep moving one place over in the circle, when all of a sudden I started leaving little puddles of diarrhea behind where I had just been sitting. One kid after another began sitting in my fragrant little smudges, and then all hell broke loose. I realized that it was no use; I would be found out. So I just let go – and I mean let go. I exploded; kids were screaming and the teacher tried to remain calm as she wrapped me in an emergency fire blanket to stop the shit from flying all over the room. She then threw me over her shoulder and headed down the school hallway to the nurse's office. I remember seeing all of these older kids in the hallway, and here I was unceremoniously hurled over some lady's back being carted across the school, a stinky little package of embarrassment. To top it all off my brothers vehemently denied any relation to me as the story was told and retold throughout the school for what seemed like years. I was the little girl who exploded like a giant shit balloon. Luckily my father got transferred back to Connecticut soon afterwards.

I say luckily, but the trip was a living hell, as were all our family trips. Let me tell you, shoving a bunch of related people into an unairconditioned car in the middle of a hot, sticky summer, and then having them travel to someplace as mind-numbingly boring as the Liberty Bell is no picnic. I don't know whose big idea the cross-country family vacation was, but I can attest to the raw, unadulterated horror of it.

Many a childhood summer was spent dumped into the back seat of the family car, usually something large and American with a "Buy American or bye-bye America" bumper sticker plastered on the back just to drive the point home. Oh how I yearned to be alone in the cool sanctuary of the fragrant woods behind our house, reading my beloved books or pretending to be on TV.

If my brothers were lucky they could stay home from these trips and throw teenage sex parties while the family poodle and I sweated on the faux leather seat and desperately held our bladders for weeks on end. I'd always had a tendency of overpacking for even a trip to the grocery store. Convinced that a car accident would land us on a planet with no food or water or a sudden snowstorm would leave us naked and freezing to death, I brought along my trusty little suitcase/survival kit every time I left the house. It contained a change of clothes, a warm sweater, snacks, a few books and games, a drink or two, Kleenex, gum, money, and a crossword puzzle. I was three when I started doing this. No one seemed to think it odd. In fact, I was looked on admirably and was much appreciated when someone was thirsty or bored. However when I look back at it now I think that either a) I really wanted to get the hell out of there fast, b) I was petrified of being left alone and having to fend for myself, or c) I was deeply mistrustful of my parent's ability to drive safely. I don't know, I guess any of those choices spell "insecure" to me, and you have to wonder why none of the adults in my life took notice.

On the occasions when my brothers would grace us with their presence on the "family vacation," what was usually un-bearable became a madness-inducing, American-made, rolling torture chamber for me. Surrounded by three boys all a year apart in age and with just the tinge of prepubescent funk on them, I was in puerile hell.

Stupid jokes, pinching until purple and black welts dotted my fair skin, spittle in my hair, chewing gum on my books, any-thing and everything to drive me closer to insanity. My mother speaks glowingly and nostalgically when remembering what a sweet, quiet child I was. That wasn't quiet Ma, it was shell-shock! I was just trying to be as small and invisible as humanly possible so the trio of simians your loins threw into the world wouldn't notice me.

My God, it was hell! Once in awhile my father would grow sick of the sound of abuse and fling one long, hairy arm in the general direction of the back seat and shout "God dammiit PatrickJimmyVincent stop touching your sister!" at which point one of the trio would stick a filthy, squirming little finger a na-nometer away from my face and mock me saying, "I'm not touching you, I'm not touching you." Oh the sophomoric hu-mor ran rampant! Who could blame me for burying my nose in Laura Ingalls Wilder books? Who could blame me for reading over two hundred books in one summer?

I needed to escape, and books were my ticket to the world. Books and my imagination carried me through my formative years. I don't recall the Liberty Bell or The Alamo or any of the other places that we visited, but I sure do remember the car trips, the rest stops, and Ma and Pa Ingalls.

Back in the 70's food was pretty basic in the states. You had Shake and Bake chicken for dinner with some Tater Tots and an iceberg lettuce salad with Good Seasons salad dressing on it. And that was considered a "home cooked" meal. Well, the food on the road made that look damn good.

Howard Johnson's seemed to be my Dad's idea of the perfect stop. I know it was cheap, and he had four kids, but my Lord if I ever see another "smiley face" breakfast again I will go on a shooting rampage. In case you've never experienced the breakfast of death, it consisted of one doughy, enormous, tasteless pancake with two greasy fried eggs as the eyes and a strip of undercooked bacon as the mouth, curled into a greasy grin. Then you got the "butter," which was whipped lard, on the side, a serving the size of a scoop of ice cream, and a selection of syrups, none of which came from Vermont or had ever even been near a tree. Things like Boysenberry delight! Or Maple Magic! Sugar and flavorings boiled down and stuck in glass canisters that were occasionally wiped down with a filthy rag brandished by one of the beehive topped waitresses. Watery coffee, thinned-down frozen orange juice, and odd-tasting ice water filled out the dining experience. I am convinced that being exposed to the horrors of Howard Johnson's at such an early age is what has made me the food snob that I am today… Well, when I'm not forced to eat a bag of peanut M and M's and a diet soda as a meal.

Westport, Connecticut was a good place to grow up. The town had a mini bus that would take you downtown for 50 cents. On Main Street you could shoplift stupid trinkets from "The Party Shop" or look for books at the hot pink painted "Remarkable" book shop – it was a Democratic voting booth last time I was there. You could also see a movie for $2.50 and get a slice of pizza and a drink at the fabulous Westport Pizzeria. The local deli deli was run by a bitter man who felt ripped off by local Westport movie star Paul Newman. See, he had signed on to help Paul's nonprofit with food stuffs and didn't make any money off it. Apparently the moron didn't understand what the term "nonprofit" meant… anyway, he had great pickles and rye bread.

I spent a lot of time with other tall girls; we were the Amazon squad. Anne the brainy one, Suzy the unattractive one, Keri, the beautiful athlete… We could have filled out the cast for an after-school special.

The one person I hated in school was an ugly little girl named Nancy who always got the leads in all the school shows. I admit that she had a better voice than I did, but boy was it tough to suck it up every time she got a big role and I was relegated to the frigging chorus. My big break came when I was in eighth grade; I finally got a great role in the Gershwin show as a Dolly sister. When I saw the photos my dad had taken of me, I realized that I was no longer a complete dog. It was very exciting and confidence building. I got to wear short shorts and high heels; my mom recalls my long legs and how the makeup made me look pretty, but then my mom always told me I looked good, in spite of the fact that she was a goddess and I looked like the fourth boy until I was fourteen.

We used to go to a store called Hit or Miss to buy new school clothes for me. My mom had always been a clothes-horse, and we would get great piles of stuff and then take all of the price tags off and leave the bags in the trunk if my dad was home so he wouldn't yell at my mom. If dad noticed something we were wearing and asked if it was new we would say… "No, I've had it for ages," or I would say that one of my rich friends gave it to me.

The rich kids went on vacations to Jamaica and the Bahamas, and their dads were doctors and drove Mercedes. Most of them were Jewish. The average-middle class kids were like us, and some of the kids were poor and would wear pants that were too short and ratty tennis shoes. I felt sorry for those kids who were going to such an elitist school. At least my mom dressed me so I looked like we had a yacht, not a Boston Whaler. I even won best-dressed one year in the yearbook.

I had my first real boyfriend, Roger, in the seventh grade; he was a year ahead of me and was an incredibly talented young man. He played piano and drew amazing portraits, wrote music and poetry. I broke up with him after a long and melodramatic courtship where his mother would listen in on our phone conversations – she was an utter bitch.

We'd very responsibly discussed and then actually did go to

second base. I remember getting my little booby felt up at a make out party in some kid's basement one night and feeling so grown up about it. Now I just go to Morocco and perfect strangers feel me up while I'm shopping.

When I was 14 we were transferred to Southern California, a move which I was convinced was ordained by the heavens for one reason and one reason only – so that I could become a movie star. One slight problem was the fact that we moved to Orange County, not Los Angeles County, but that didn't stop me from planning my escape. I did high school in three years instead of four and worked at odd jobs and modeling to earn enough cash to move out.

I got kicked out of drama class, but the teacher had flames tattooed out of his butt and armpits, so his taste was obviously a bit dodgy.

It must have really burned his ass when I won a drama scholarship. The Laguna Beach playhouse held the competition, and I joined it and won by doing a scene from *Bus Stop*, Marilyn Monroe's part. I never actually used my scholarship because by eighteen I was starring in the first of many TV series, so college didn't make sense for me – though I do encourage any kid reading this to a) Not use foul language like I do, and b) get as much education as your folks will spring for.

I left home young and began to seek my fortune. I met an old actor from a TV series that ran in the 70s. He hit on me while I was working in a restaurant in Laguna Beach and only laid off when I told him I was underage. He introduced me to an old writer who used to bang all the old Hollywood ladies and told me he was blackballed during the McCarthy era. That writer introduced me to my first manager; a frightening woman named Joan who used to weigh me in her office and always dressed in inappropriate clothes for a woman her age.

She was a high-strung, neurotic woman, but she got me in the union by setting up a general meeting with Irene Mariano at Lorimar before my eighteenth birthday. She liked me and gave me five lines on *Dallas* so I could get my SAG card. After that I must have been put on a list of some sorts because I did *Falcon Crest* and then *Berringers* and on and on. I worked a ton in TV and had a great time. I suddenly could afford a nice apartment and a new car – life was good.

In 1986 I was cast in my first film, *The Hidden*, a New Line Cinema film directed by Jack Sholder. I played a stripper who gets taken over by a male alien. Some other gal had the part originally, but something went wrong so I went up for it. I knew they wanted big boobs, but I was really skinny and had a small chest, so I stuffed my bathing suit top. They weren't very happy when I showed up at work and couldn't do the scene topless as planned, but they built a lovely set of prosthetic breasts into my dress and all was well. My outfits in that movie were amazing, a buttless dress, thigh-high red boots, and a faux monkey fur trimmed coat. I felt like I was on Soul Train!

After *The Hidden* I went up for the female lead in *Clean and Sober*, a part I wanted desperately. I really liked the director, Glenn Gordon Caron, and I did a really good reading. I was told a few weeks later that I was too young and too pretty, but would I do the smaller role of Iris? I told my agent that I would do an extra role if it meant working with Michael Keaton and Morgan Freeman. I had a great time, and Cathy Baker was, as always, fantastic in the role I went up for originally. Morgan Freeman was very generous to work with, he told me that my eyes were extremely expressive and would keep me working forever – very kind words to say to a young kid just starting out.

I spent the 80s and 90s working with lots of interesting people. I was the ingénue in a film with Bob Hope, Don Ameche, Yvette Mimieux, Ann Francis, Frank Gorshin and other greats. I worked with Sharon Stone in a cheesy movie of the week called *Calendar Girl Murders* produced by Steve Tisch, who would go on to *Forrest Gump* success. During this time I dated studio head's sons, European princes, Middle Eastern billionaires, and all sorts of actors. It was a heady time being young and pretty and hanging out at Spago when it was still up on the hill, Nippers in Beverly Hills, Helena's in Silver Lake, and Tramp under the Beverly Center. I made out with super models and rock stars and still managed to be a good girl, married at 23 and faithful… but I wasn't married long. I divorced my husband Gary Devore at 26.

Gary's death – years after our divorce – is listed as one of Hollywood's most mysterious with a number of stories being circulated about how and why. My old best friend Lana Clarkson was killed by Phil Spector. My ex-boyfriend Dodi Fayed died in the car with Princess Diana, and too many people I know have disappeared.

I feel blessed to be here and happy and healthy, and all of this leads me up to a fateful day when I was in my twenties and got a phone call from my agent saying that I had an audition the next day for a Sci-Fi show called *Babylon 5*.

Ivanova Is God

I went in at noon and met with JMS, John Copland, and Doug
Netter. They asked me to read a scene that had Ivanova acting
very tough and sarcastic to Garibaldi. I read the scene, they
said thank you, we made a little small talk, and that was that.
They then asked me if I could come back at 3:00 PM and do it
again. I went back, did the same thing all over again, and then
left.

My agent and I had a discussion about the fact that it was a
five year commitment, and she said something to the effect of,
"Well, I doubt it will last more than a year seeing as no Sci-Fi
shows other than *Star Trek* ever do."

This was true back then. *Star Trek* and their spin-offs had
the Sci-Fi market to themselves. I thought about it and decided
that the writing was good, the character strong and interesting,
and that if they wanted me, I would do it.

They wanted me. In spite of the rumors of Iman being
offered the role and all sorts of other garbage I was told, they
offered me the role very soon after the audition.

I didn't realize that they had already made a B5 pilot with a
different gal in the lead, so it was a bit of a shock to see it.
Tamilyn Tomito was too short to play with the guys; that's what
I was told anyway. Suddenly my height and authoritative de-
meanor were appreciated, and I was, for the first time in my
career, not told to "soften up" the character. Joy!

The first season was a bit of a cluster for a lot of people,
frankly. No one got on with the lead guy, and rumors of sexual
harassment suits and other shenanigans abounded. I was having a great time, though. I loved the crew and made friends
with many of the cast members and production staff. We shot
in an old warehouse next to an Orange Bang! factory. The sets

were kind of flimsy the first season, with walls on which you could see the seams and a command deck that looked as if it came in a box under the Christmas tree.

The uniforms were hideous the first season. They were wool, and we shot in the San Fernando Valley where 90 degrees was a normal summer day. My shirt was a one-piece body suit with snaps in the crotch – always a nuisance. The slacks inevitably made me look like I had a pot belly and showed the men's nether regions as well – not fun. Between me trying to flatten my gut and O'Hare arranging his junk every other minute, I was began to despise those uniforms with a passion. The only thing worse was the flying outfit for the Starfurys. They were like the Michelin Man on acid. I felt like I was wearing a diving suit from Communist Russia circa 1950. I swam in the boots, couldn't drop my arms to my sides, the helmet would steam up after two seconds, so you had to have a fan on between takes so you couldn't hear anyone – it was not fun. Not to mention the fact that after putting you in this restraint they then buckled you into a fake cockpit.

One of the larger of the Northridge earthquake's aftershocks hit while I was strapped into the cockpit. Everyone ran out of the studio to safety and left me dangling there in fear for my life. Luckily my intrepid prop master, Kurt, hurried back to untangle and rescue me.

I remember a fellow named Eric who was a man of all jobs on the set. Off the set he raised and cared for wolves. He brought one to the set the day of the aftershock, and she was chained up outside. The only time she ever made a sound was right before the quake – she howled. Very eerie.

I forgave my selfish costars and crew for abandoning me in my time of need, and things got back to normal.

O'Hare was replaced by a nervous and sweet Bruce Boxleitner, who very quickly became my hero. I was so thrilled to be working with someone sane, nice, easy, and professional that I could hardly believe my luck. Suddenly the vibe on the set became harmonious, and work was once again a complete joy.

B5 had a very civilized schedule, for the humans, that is. I usually got to work between 6 and 8am and finished at 8pm with a half hour lunch around one o'clock. In the morning I got a cup of tea, or someone brought me one into the makeup trailer, and I would sit and get my hair and makeup done. Most days this process took about a half hour. I wore a ponytail 95 percent of the time. It wasn't until the third season that they started to get fancy with my tail, trying all sorts of weird braids and crap, which I thought was ridiculous for Ivanova to have. She never would have fussed in the mirror that long. Makeup was minimal. I wore a little base and some blush, mascara, and a light lip liner with Chap Stick over it. I had a tiny bit of eye pencil on in some episodes, and we played with eye shadows when we were bored or when I was dressed in something other than the uniform.

For the few times I wore my hair down we played like little girls with curling irons, hot rollers, and all sorts of stuff. I rarely felt glamorous except on those days – the negligee and hair down episodes.

And why did they dress Ivanova up? Well, at least in part it was because of a barrage of letters from fans requesting to see me in something other than the uniform and a ponytail. Shame on all of you! Actually it was nice having scenes that did not take place in C and C for a change.

People always ask me which episodes were my favorites. I don't even have to think about it. I most enjoyed the episodes where I could express emotion or make people laugh. The Drazi episode, sitting Shiva for my father with Uncle Yossel, Sleeping in Light, the fight scenes and Starfury battles... they were all fun or challenging, which makes for an interesting day at work.

The camaraderie on the set was truly unique and a complete joy to be a part of, though the actors did tend to gravitate towards each other as far as humans and aliens went. The aliens spent so much time together in makeup they had a completely different experience than the humans had. The alien makeup trailer was a peaceful place with mellow music on and no talking. The actors would sometimes try to sleep or just relax while the makeup was applied at the UN-Godly hours of 3:00 or 4:00 AM.

The human trailer on the other hand was a raucous place with the poor makeup and hair people trying to wrangle us into our seats like a bunch of kindergardeners on speed. Here we were all jacked up on caffeine, ready to start the day, and resenting having to put makeup on. I think I am one of the few actresses on the planet who actually prefers not to be touched up or powdered or even have makeup on in the first place, it drives me nuts!

I sometimes felt badly for the guest stars and co-stars on our show because there were so many inside jokes and high jinx among the cast and crew that I thought they must have felt as if they had walked into the wrong wedding party. We tried our best to make people feel at ease, and I would like to think that they had a good experience on the show, but there was definitely a club-like atmosphere among the regulars.

The first convention I recall was in the UK, and I brought my mother with me. We were doing it as a publicity stunt for the show. None of us knew that someday people would actually pay for the photos we were signing and giving away for free! My mother was in a state of shock over the length of the line of people waiting for our autographs, it snaked around the corner and down into a hallway and never ended.

This would be the beginning of the phenomenon of *Babylon 5*, the little show which took on the biggest Sci-Fi franchise to date. At half the budget and no fan base, we were an anomaly, but I realized when I saw all of those people happily standing in line that we were on to something, and that Sci-Fi fans had to be the most loyal fans I had ever seen in my life!

Muse to the Geeks

People often ask me what makes Sci-Fi fans or genre fans so unique. I have to say that it is a myriad of things. Loyal, inno-cent, enthusiastic, interesting, intelligent, silly, fun and bizarre... and that's just the kids!

I'll give you an example of the "loyalty factor." It was the days post Al Gore's presidential theft, and the LA Times had an article asking people to vote for their choice of person to host the Oscars that year. My fans were cajoled by a brilliant Holly Evans, and I won the popular vote by a landslide. Of course, like Gore, I never got to fill my elected position. I did end up the focus of the article however! Thanks to the fans who wrote in!

A few years back I was developing a pilot with another ac-tress and we made a website to show the potential investors that we had "fan power." We then asked people to hit the site and garnered over a million hits in a few days – now that's loy-alty.

I find the fact that large groups of people can peacefully gather in various venues to celebrate their love of certain TV shows, films, comics and books... refreshing to say the least. Sci-Fi fans in general are not violent, do not drink or take drugs excessively, (though Mead and Romulan ale abuse does abound). I have not witnessed many fights or arguments amongst the fans, and I have not seen them abuse their children or spouses.

Yes, I have seen silly arguments and anger at the people throwing the events when the fans feel abused or taken advan-tage of. But in general I see a lot of people simply gathering and enjoying themselves much like I used to do at Renaissance fairs and musical events.

Of course there are always a few people who will throw a damper on conventions – attention getters and jerks – but hey, you can find that type in everyday life as well, and considering the size of some of these conventions and how many I have done, I have witnessed surprisingly few incidents that weren't easily handled.

I have had good times and bad times at conventions. I have met people who have become friends for life, lovers, and one-night stands at conventions. One never knows what can happen on one of these crazy weekends, but I hope to share with you a few stories from the last decade of my life.

At a con in 1994 I met a young lady named Holly Evans. Her girlfriend loved B5, and had dragged her to the convention. Holly very sweetly presented me with a stained glass panel she had made depicting the B5 logo and my character's name. I thought it was a very nice gesture and, not having been raised in a barn, I sent Miss Evans a thank you note upon returning to LA. Apparently this was very un-TV star like behavior, because she was absolutely shocked. I was one of only two people who had ever acknowledged such a gift. We became friendly, and by the time I went to 1996 Visions in Chicago, Illinois, I had decided to ask Holly to start booking conventions for me.

Prior to Holly I'd had a few different people helping me out. One was my oldest friend Damon, who had experienced six weeks in a car with me driving across Germany from convention to convention. Let's just say that the fact that we are still friends is a testament to the fact that we are both afflicted with the inability to recall places and events. Six weeks in a car with anyone, driving in Germany, staying in crappy B and B's and eating nothing but meat and cheese because you are both on the Atkins' diet… is enough to put a damper on any friendship. Trust me on this one.

The German fiasco was a bad time in my life. A time when I honestly believed that Sci-Fi conventions would be a great way to see the world. They are NOT a great way to see the world. Unless you stay an extra week or two and use it as a launching pad to a holiday, they are a long weekend of work in an exotic location, period. It's still a Holiday Inn, just with a tropical theme. The food is still hotel food, and you are grateful for it at 2:00 AM when the masquerade-disco party is FINALLY over.

One must understand the reality of these events. A few months for someone like Holly to organize the flights, hotel rooms, fees (if there are any) per diem, contracts etc. Then you pack and fly to wherever the event is. Then you do the event, repack, fly home and recuperate from the jet lag. That's the disappointment and the sheer insanity of doing conventions. If I had a nickel for every time I heard an actor say, "I will never do another con again," I would be living in Italy with my pool boy and a housekeeper named Lucia.

I am not saying that some conventions have not been fun. There have been the occasional jolly ones. I am not saying that I have not made stupid money at some of these cons. I am just saying that there is something inherently soul-sucking huckster-like about sitting at a table selling photos of yourself and signing body parts and dolls for fans of a show you are no longer working on. It's an odd mixture of pride and humiliation. You have to understand the feeling when someone recognizes you for your work on a show, which they enjoyed, but then does not understand or acknowledge that you have a very wide range of acting experience, not just "their show."

A lot of fans of B-5 don't care if you did the Edinburgh Festival, worked with your favorite Indie director, or booked a sit-com. They want you back on "the show"!!!! And they want to watch new episodes of that show with YOU in it! So, you see it's a kinda lose-lose situation... but still fun at times, which is why we keep coming back.

Holly started booking conventions for me, and we had some interesting experiences. There was Chiller Theatre where she almost got killed by a tent, which collapsed, and I was stuck next to a woman who was screaming so loud that I could not hear for the rest of the con. We did a Shore Leave once where we met some fans who had musical talent, and we all sat up in the bar until three in the morning singing Beatle's songs, that was fun, and I realized in hindsight that the management of the hotel had been very kind.

At the Chicago Comicon Holly and I went to Morton's Steak House after work one night and had the best meal we had ever had at a convention! Big, fat, juicy steaks, and spinach and mushrooms, mashed potatoes, and a gigantic chocolate cake all washed down with a bottle of fine California Cabernet; we could hardly walk back to the hotel. There was Eroticon in New Orleans where Holly and I discovered pot brownies accidentally and tripped the whole weekend. They were really strong and tasty, and being chocolate fans we ate way too many before realizing what they were. I was very friendly that weekend, more so than usual. We kept giggling at everything before it dawned on me that the breakfast spread was not really that amusing, and something must be wrong with us. I recalled the person who had the brownies and it all clicked; I was stoned at 9:00 am with an equally stoned person working my table. It was a challenge of a day.

I did Dragon*Con a few times, but the most memorable one for me was one where I had to introduce a tiny sprite of a singer named Apollo Smile for a concert they were doing. The bands were running late, and I was tired and wanted to end my day. It was around 11 P.M., I was sick of waiting, and the band on stage was simply awful. I waited and waited, and then finally I snapped. I went on stage and asked the audience if they really wanted to hear anymore of this crap, and they shouted "NO!" So I booted the band off and introduced Apollo Smile, who made everyone much happier. She could have taken the stage and read the Koran and made people happier – the previous band was that bad. Now, I realized that this was not a terribly nice thing for me to do, and I felt bad for a moment. However, the band members acted as if I had killed their mascot, the rare wood owl. I had young, dirty, longhaired, smelly, grungy, faux-band members yelling at me and shoving their black-painted nails in my face. I got grief for the rest of the time I was there and eventually had to sit down with one of them and tell them that I was sorry, but they sucked, and I was tired of waiting, and they sucked and, well, they sucked. I was not going to back down from the fact that they sucked. Sorry, they sucked. There I said it; they sucked.

Since I am visiting some bad memories let's just dive right in and go to THE WORST CONVENTION EVENT IN THE UNIVERSE! "Claudia gets shot by a Tribble."

This is a true story.

I had been receiving crazy-colored, hand-knitted items for a while from a fellow we shall call "M." M worked for the post office (I am not making this up) and was a keen Sci-Fi fan and B5 enthusiast. M would send me packages with little home-made tea cozy's and doilies which he knit himself whilst sitting in his postal truck (still not making this up). I sent back thank you notes like a good little girl, and received a note from him saying that he was finally going to meet me at a convention that Slanted Fedora was throwing in upstate NY, and that he had a gift for me. Well, the excitement was just beginning!

I was sitting at my table on Saturday, signing things for folks and having a pleasant time, when a very large Tribble approached my table holding an enormous black plastic garbage bag. I greeted the Tribble, and the person in the Tribble suit said that he had a gift for me. Out of the bag came a HUGE afghan in hot pink, lime green, purple and white. It was big enough to cover a California King Size bed, easy. It was massive, and very bright, and seriously belonged in Haight Ashbury in 1969 in a commune with people on acid – who would have appreciated it. I on the other hand had to pull out my finest acting skills to enthuse over the hand-made beauty, the colors, and the finesse which went into making this piece of art. I complimented and thanked, and he preened and glowed, and eventually the pre-sentation was over, the item moved to the green room, and I regained my breath and went back to signing.

M promised another gift and a surprise. I could hardly wait! What a day this was turning out to be! A dayglow afghan the size of Rhode Island and more to come!? *I'm being spoiled!* I thought.

About an hour later I spotted yet another giant Tribble lumbering towards me. This one had been altered slightly into a more menacing-looking Tribble, with wires attached to its head and red lights flashing about its furry body. It was a scary Tribble. This Tribble still had the afghan knitting- postal worker lurking beneath it, and he clearly had some unfinished business. He came straight up to the table and said "I am a morphed Tribble, now you will be morphed, too!" He then reached under his Tribble suit, into some hidden Tribble weapon arsenal, pulled out a very real-looking untribble-like gun and shot me.

Now, the thoughts which raced through my mind are not only tragic but also frankly painful for me to recall. I thought "I can see the headline now 'Babylon 5 star shot by Tribble, Sci-Fi actress meets ironic death.' This cannot be happening to me. I am supposed to die a dignified death, in bed, clutching my Oscar and my Screen Actor's Guild Award!" I was lying on the ground clutching the very painful area of my ribs where the bullet had hit and thinking dark thoughts as security dragged the morphed, psycho Tribble-killer away.

After a few moments I realized that there was no blood, and that I was very much alive. Alive and pissed off! I dusted myself off and stood up. Pulling my shirt up, I saw a reddening, nasty-looking bruise and a fat welt beginning to rise. It turned out that the gun was real, though the bullets, thankfully, were blanks. Blanks of the same caliber that killed Jon Eric Hexum and Brandon Lee. Blanks which, had they hit flesh without bone protecting it, could have damaged an internal organ or killed me.

Later in the day I received yet another garbage bag. This one had two matching hand-knitted pillows in it. I guess with all of the excitement over shooting me, he had forgotten to present me with the second part of the gift. M was banned from Slanted Fedora conventions, but that was not the end of the story. CUT TO:

November 2006, United Fan Con, Springfield, Massachusetts.

Almost a decade had gone by since my little incident with M the Tribble, and I had been warned that he would most likely be at this convention. Various fans that were privy to the story had been huddling around kindly warning me and throwing protective, furtive glances around looking for the enemy. The convention had kindly provided me with a very large bodyguard named Tiny (why, oh why are they always named Tiny or Red?), and I had my then boyfriend sitting with me at my table. We were all fully prepared for the second attack. I grabbed my boyfriend's knee and whispered "There he is!" when I saw the familiar face. No costume this time, just unkempt hair and a pair of ratty old slippers – normal for cons. He approached the table, I tensed, my boyfriend tensed, Tiny raised himself even higher and puffed out his formidable chest, and M says, wait for it... yes, he actually says... "I bet you don't remember me."

I kid you not. I stared at him in complete amazement, and after a beat I said, "Oh, I remember you all right... You shot me."

He looked stunned, then scratched his head as if trying to recall what he ate for breakfast, then he finally brightened up and responded, "Oh yeah! I shot you!"

Now ladies and gentlemen, try to imagine a life so rich and varied, so full of surprises and excitement, that you cannot re-member shooting an actress at a Sci-Fi convention, being dragged away from the scene of the crime by four giants, physi-cally removed from the property, and banned for life. This M fellow has surely won the lottery of life if that event was forget-table. Sadly it will stay with me for the rest of my days.

Nothing dramatic happened at that convention with my old buddy M the postal worker; however, I did watch my back and my front more than usual that weekend.

I have done shows in foreign countries where they did not provide translators for the Q and A's. I have had checks bounce on me from promoters from all over this great planet. I have had people tattoo my signature on their body, legally change their name to Susan Ivanova, and I can list at least a dozen stalkers through the years. I have had fans — both male and female — become overly enamored with me, and I have the restraining orders to prove it.

Which brings me to Las Vegas 1997. I was with Damon, our cop-friend Kevin, and a few Las Vegas police officers, huddled in a corner of a large-venue room sipping coffee and explaining the situation to the cops. A man with a rather tenuous grasp on reality had been sending love letters and flowers to me at my P.O. Box in Hollywood. He had written of his plan to sell his house, quit his job, and move to LA so that we could be together. After all, we were married in the world he had created in his mind. His sister confirmed all of this and was quite concerned about his mental health. "You think, Sis? Gee, I just thought it was a harmless crush!" Apparently he HAD indeed quit his job, sold his house, and his sister and family had no idea where he was. I did. Needless to say I was frightened, and after months of dealing with this fruitcake, not being able to pick up my mail for fear he was waiting at the P.O. Box, etc. etc., I was more than ready to see the back of him.

A bit of back story; Damon and Kevin had taken in a very young Aussie gal and had let her stay at their apartment. She had seen a photo of the stalker guy once. She was at the convention looking at comic books; she was barely old enough to drive.

Okay, the cops knew what the guy looked like since he conveniently sent me a photo for my bedside. We were all prepped and ready to nab this guy! Damon and Kevin had fancy-looking headgear, lots of walkie-talkies, guns, and all sorts of macho crap. One takes up a position behind me while the other one keeps watch on the perimeter of my table. I am signing and focusing on the fans. A few hours go by when all of a sudden, the Aussie girl-child comes up to me and points to a man about an inch away from me and says, "Isn't that the stalker, mate?"

"Yes, it is the stalker, mate, and thank you so much."

She said the guy had been circling my table for about an hour, and she was wondering when they were going to nab him.

She thought it would be cool to be close up when it went down. Apparently half a dozen cops and two bodyguards fitted out for the sequel to the Matrix couldn't see the fellow, but a pubescent foreigner recognized him from a brief glance at a photo two days prior.

Suddenly walkies screeched, bodies tumbled, and the cops ran in and handcuffed the guy and dragged him away. Unbeknownst to me, that would be the closest I would come to being married for the rest of my life thus far.

I found out later that his excuse for harassing me was my fault actually, or at least it was in his twisted little brain. I had apparently left my wedding ring on the sink of our kitchen prior to flying to Vegas, and he was simply being a good husband and returning it to me. I wish I was making this stuff up.

Other than violent Star Trek characters and stalkers, I have met some pretty bizarre people at conventions. A lot of them claim to be "amazing" at many things. Amazing masseuses for instance. I have had some of the worst rubs at cons, and some of the best, and it's really hard to tell who's going to suck until you're sitting down with someone's hands on your neck and you realize, *What the fuck am I doing? They could choke me; wait they ARE choking me! Oh, that's their "style"!*

I remember being at a convention with Holly. We were burnt out; it was a long weekend, and we'd worked hard. Sunday night a fellow who had been making frequent visits to my table offered his services as a masseuse. We said fine just because we were so knackered and clearly incapable of reasonable thought. Not only did we say yes, but we also complied when he said that it would be better and easier in one of our rooms. We agreed to meet at the end of the day at my table. Holly and I packed up and the fellow helped us carry the boxes to Holly's room. I said that I would be back in a minute and went to get a drink and clean up while Holly got her massage. I used my key about a half hour later and found Holly buckassed naked on the bed and this guy was rubbing her butt like he was churning butter! I couldn't help it; I burst out in laughter and couldn't stop for a good ten minutes. Needless to say I did not get a massage that evening.

People have read my palm, thrown runes, and performed Tarot card readings. I have also used my magical psychic powers – which only come out after copious amounts of alcohol – on many fans. In fact, Holly and I were in Boston during an event and I met a gal at the bar – where else? – and began to read her palm. I don't remember much of what I said, but apparently I told her to quit her job, go to art school, and make amends with her father because he was not long for the world. God's honest truth, about a year later we received an email from this gal. She had quit her job, was happily in art school and had already booked some work as a graphic designer. She made up with her dad, and he passed away a few months later leaving her enough money to stay in school and pursue her dreams. She was happy and in love and thanked me for changing her life. It's moments like that when I wonder why I quit drinking.

In Houston I did a convention and got to visit my brother's grave. Patrick died in 1973, hit by a car while riding his bike. We moved back to Connecticut a few months after he was killed, but we didn't bring his body with us, he was stuck in a place he hated and the place he died. This has never sat well with any of us, and the idea of moving him has been brought up from time to time over the years. My parents are too old now, and divorced as well, so the subject no longer arises.

I met Wallis, one of my mother's oldest friends who still lives in Houston, and we ate at a Mexican joint, had a few margaritas, and drove to the cemetery. I sort of recognized it. I was eight years old when we buried him, and I recall putting a pocket knife he had always coveted into his grave. I remember wishing I had given it to him when he was alive. I didn't need it; he was a boy who loved being outdoors, so he should have had it. I thought that perhaps if he had won the straw draw and won the knife, maybe he would still be alive. Maybe he would have been playing with the knife out in the woods, digging up mushrooms or something instead of riding around on his bike, waiting to be hit. I guess everyone goes through the "what ifs" and "maybes" when someone they love dies. It's a horrible thing when a child dies, hard on the parents and hard on the siblings. It instantly changes the dynamic of your family and the quality of your life... forever.

We got lost looking for Pat's grave and wandered around for a while; I recalled that it was under a tree and near a fence where there were horses. The freeway now encroached and practically backed up into my brother's gravesite. Thirty years is a long time, I realized. We found the overgrown plaque and I cleaned it off, photographed it, cried a bit and lay down on top of his grave trying to feel something. There was nothing. That beautiful, poet spirit which was my brother had moved on a long, long time ago and all that was left here was his name and some dust. I realized that he would never be moved and that he was already long gone from this grave and even longer from this planet.

One has to look for positives in life. I met Selina Rosen and Michael Stackpole on that trip. Michael and I were friendly for a while, and Selina and I still to this day are friends and collaborators. Like I said before, I have met some amazing people at conventions.

Over the years I have received many gifts from fans. Fan artwork is always fun. It's interesting to see what people really think you look like or what they think you are like as a person. I have had people draw me with lions, swords, on horseback or in full military garb. I have had people make dolls of me in various stages of dress and undress, with various hair and eye colors and some do not look even remotely like me. That's when I have to ask them "Are you sure this is me?" and they will sheepishly admit that it's Terry Farrell or some other tall, dark-haired Sci-Fi actress, but that they wanted my autograph. Okay.

I have been given a lot of food products. A fellow named John is somewhat known for pushing fudge on the ladies. He was recently informed by both Erin Gray and me that we don't really like fudge, so now we get dark chocolate instead when we see him. I have been given homemade mead, chili sauce, beer, trail mix, chocolate roses, raisins, kisses, nuts, bars, and just about everything chocolate. I have been sent homemade jams and jellies, canned fruits and vegetables, dried meats, and cookies and cakes and muffins and candy!

I have been sent or given hundreds of stuffed animals which I have donated to the children's hospital over the years. I have received Christmas ornaments, weapons and books… lot's of books. That's the neat thing about fans; they really listen to you and think hard about what to get you. The fact that I love edged weapons and books has clearly been heard because I have received all sorts of daggers, knives, swords, broad swords, pocket knives, even maces and shields! Books have come to me from all over the world. Books on subjects I love such as history, and books I would never buy for myself such as fantasy and science fiction. I have tried to read all of them, but honestly I have a few boxes to go.

Books are a fabulous offering, for they provide an insight to the giver as well as the receiver… hence my extensive collection of books on vampires and dragons from my fans. I will try and crack those someday as well.

Back in the early days we were all pretty wild. I have heard stories about my co-star's behavior on cruises, and I am sure that they have heard tales of my late-night sing alongs in bars across the country. It's a funny thing what happens in the life of a convention attendee. You start out sort of enjoying the attention and the easy money, and then you end up resenting the events and the travel and the demanding, rude fans and organizers at some events. Some weekends are peaceful and a breeze and others are nightmarish and chock full o' drama. There are disorganized events where you want to strangle the people who threw the convention and others where you are treated nicely, picked up on time, and don't have to hunt down your per diem. There are some people who have been banned from throwing cons, some who are downright hated, and a handful who are in jail.

There are difficult actors and actresses, moody writers, directors, and comic book people. There are vendors who don't want to be there and dealers who have lost their ass at the convention and don't have money for gas home. With all of these scenarios you must also figure in the multitude of different personalities. I have been tired at times or had to deal with an obnoxious fan or a difficult promoter, but I have always tried to be polite and funny and to make the fans feel like they have met a decent person who cares about them.

I do not understand performers who show up at events and just sit there rolling their eyes at the fans or not making eye contact and generally behaving like boobs. It sucks, and it shouldn't be tolerated. Those people should not be invited to cons, and it is up to the fans to make that clear. Unfortunately, a lot of fans will put up with that kind of behavior in order to get an autograph that they want, so the jerks keep coming back and treating people like crap.

I played with a koala bear in Australia in 2006 and nipped off to Paris to do a con for a lovely lady named Pascale. I have been able to visit friends in Hawks Bay, New Zealand thanks to a con, and I have seen a huge amount of Germany as well. In Tel Aviv I had an amazing time in 2005. I attended a very small convention due to the planning and perseverance of a young man named Oded. I didn't realize that B5 was so popular in Israel, and was treated like a princess. In one restaurant I was sent drinks and food and eventually a gorgeous young waiter got the courage to speak to me. He told me that I was "the last woman who could have kept him from going gay," needless to say I was heartbroken I didn't get to him in time! I also discovered the beautiful beaches of Tel Aviv, spent Passover at Oded's parents' home eating a traditional Passover meal and being stared at by his Bubby who couldn't figure out, who was the *shiksa* sharing their table.

After living in London for a few years where no one makes eye contact with you, I was also surprised at the staring going on in Israel! Everyone checks you out, male and female, just like Romanians! I have never been so stared at in my life as I was in Tel Aviv and in Bucharest.

On the way home I was stopped in the airport. The Tel Aviv airport has an understandably strict luggage search, and I had passed through the fourth of about six steps of the interrogation process when suddenly I was pulled out of the line, my passport was seized, and I was sent to a corner. I watched as a bunch of uniformed guards huddled around pointing and arguing. Then they forgot about me and I waited, confused. I did not want to push my luck, but my plane was going to leave, so I politely inquired about my passport and my luggage and was told to basically shut up and stand in the corner. I went through my luggage in my head. I knew that the hot rollers had caused confusion on the way in, maybe they were still suspect? I had no food, nothing which could be used as a weapon, and no dangerous-looking liquids. My passport was up to date, but it did have a South African stamp in it, did they hate South Africa? Maybe there was a problem with me having an American accent and a British work permit? Perhaps President Bush did something stupid again? My mind was reeling when, after some time, a woman came to me holding my passport like it was a turd and asked me to follow her. We passed all of the normal passengers being frisked and asked questions and went through a metal detector and another door and eventually came to be standing in front of the gate for my flight!

The guard handed me my passport, another woman handed me a boarding pass, and they wished me well. I looked at my boarding pass, seat 1A. All of the fuss and fear was because they had sweetly, covertly, upgraded me. God Bless Israel.

Israel Trip
Olamot, 2006

Top: Dean, Hagai Jacobson, me, and Aviv
(ducking behind me)
Bottom: Dean practising his "long, far-away" gaze
with a cute fan

"Bad shirts can happen to cute guys."

Israel Trip
Olamot, 2006

Top: Aviv in the "bad shirt."
Bottom: Hagai and me - practicing my "trout mouth" face

Israel Trip
Jerusalem, 2006

Top: Hagai, Noga
Gisis, Lee Eden
(Oded's fiancee), and
Oded Sharon (con
organizer)

Left: Dean and I

Israel Trip
Jerusalem, 2006

Top: Me and Lee
Bottom: "I'll give you two Ivanova action figures for five
strands of those beads..."

Israel Trip
Jerusalem, 2006

Top: "Plastic weapons... yay!"
Bottom: Private tour of a small museum. He recognized
me... unbelievable!

Israel Trip
Jerusalem, 2006
Top: Lee, me and Dean

Australia Trip

He didn't recognize me; he's just begging.

Feeding the giraffes espresso beans! (Just kidding, PETA.)

Australia Trip

Camels are the reason why God invented cologne - phew!

Top: Claudia and Andy Steward, NEC 2004

Ivanova is Always Right
You will listen to Ivanova
Ivanova is God

Top: Mark Spencer, Pascale, Holly and I.
Below: Richard Biggs, Kelly Dubos, and I

Bottom of previous page: I'm holding the stained glass Holly
just gave me, Holly & Dee.
Thank the heavens Holly's poodle perm and baseball sized
eyeglasses phase was fairly short lived...

"Claudia Christian's reaction when I gave her the needlework.
My brother took these pictures." -- Margret Gunn

The needlework that Margret Gunn presented to me.

Top: Michael Ryan and Claudia.

Below: Randy Maycleoch and Claudia

"Prom-con" pic!

North Dakota "06

Beware of men with ale mugs, weapons, and AC/DC hair!

Top: Far left, front - Muselta Vander. Back, second from left - Mario. Far right, front row - Denise Crosby in front of me. Behind me on far right, back row - Douglas Aurthur.

Below: Mario, Pascale, Holly and me.

Top: Rick Biggs and Mallory (my stepsister) with me.

Below: Wayne Clack and I, NEC '99

Note the only one making a goofy face is...

Australia Trip, 2006

Top: Gift store in foreign country - right on!
Bottom & top of facing page: Photo op
Bottom right: Hey, he hasn't dropped me yet!

Left:
Photos CC Style

Below: .
The result

Tour Group, Australia Trip, 2006

Susan and I
at Icon

In a galaxy
far, far away,
I had bangs!

Westchester

Two Vestial
Virgins

Pictures by
Tanya Leinard

Picture at left by
Tanya Leinard

Yet another
military-style
jacket. I sense a
trend here...

What, you don't have photos of kitties on your chest?

Left: "Who knew Armani made a suit with the same fabric as a Klingon coat...?"

Below: "I won the Klingon look-alike contest?????"

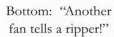

Bottom: "Another fan tells a ripper!"

Explaining quantum physics... AGAIN!
-or-
"If you buy a CD, I'll sing at your son's Bar Mitzva."

Me and a friend.

Starhyke

My grocery shopping outfit.

Artist Douglas Shuler
www.douglasshuler.com

Questions Most Commonly Asked at a Convention

Do I think this will stop fans asking them? Not really, but I might as well try.

Q. What's your favorite episode of B5?

A. Well, I would have to say that I really had fun shooting the "purple-green" Drazi episode in spite of the fact that I had just broken my foot! I broke it on a weeknight and called the producers at once so that Joe could write the accident into the next episode. I think it was a great save on his part, and the actor who played the leader of the Drazis was fantastic, the dialogue was fun, and it was one of the first times we saw Ivanova's sense of humor.

From an actress's wanting to act – point of view, "Sleeping in Light" is an absolute favorite. The scene after Marcus dies and I am with Richard Biggs crying my eyes out was so beautifully written, and my favorite director John Flynn directed it, so it was an all around good one for me. Most people don't realize that I VERY rarely had scenes with Peter or Mira or Andreas, so all of those little moments I treasured. Mira and I realized that the longest scene we ever had together one on one was in my very last episode!

When you do so many episodes – 88 – for me, there are usually a few that stand out, but in all honesty I can't recall a really bad one. Even when I was trapped in the machine down on whatever planet it was – the fans will know I'm sure – I was laughing my butt off… and anything with Zathras in it was a joy.

We were lucky to have some dynamite guest stars on our show, Robin Curtis, Tim Choate – may he rest in peace

— Ed Wasser, Robin Atkin Downes, Walter Koenig — may he finally get his star on the walk of fame — Wayne Alexander, Maggie Egan, Wortham Krimmer, Efrem Zimbalist Jr., Melissa Gilbert, and many others. They made the days fly!

Q. What's the funniest practical joke anyone ever played on anyone on B5?

A. This question always gets me…as if we all ran around with big bags of itching powder and stuck handfuls in the aliens' masks! I mean yes, we were and are a lighthearted bunch, but most of the fooling around was an everyday sort of thing. I did pull a naughty one on Jason when I told him that I had read an advance copy of a script where his character, Marcus dies… he panicked and ran around shouting and crying, and then low and behold a few episodes later, he did die. I swear I didn't know! It was just a cruel trick because he kept taking the piss out of America so we decided to exact revenge… oh well.

I also had a way of making Bill feel uncomfortable on the White Star by constantly telling him that his bone stunk, but after a long day… it really did smell like pooh, sorry Billy.

During the O.J. Simpson trial the, "human" makeup trailer was a political hot bed with Bruce and Jerry yelling and all of us arguing — man, don't ever start a political argument with Jerry Doyle, the man is frighteningly intelligent and opinionated. I loved it! We had Democrats and liberals and Republicans both conservative and not much so, so it was unsafe and volatile and exciting. The producers once asked us to sign a sexual harassment agreement basically promising that we would not leer at each other's genitals or say anything inappropriate. I don't think any of us signed it, and for the next few days we took great joy in grabbing each other's breasts and nether regions in front of the producers. Babylon 5'ers were not about to stop their flirting and sexual commentary, it's what made the days fun!

Q. What made you become an actress?

A. Well, I have always wanted to be an actress. For a brief while I wanted to be a doctor or a journalist, but I hated school and wanted to get to work immediately, so I did. It's a tough career when you are looking for work, but a wonderful one when you're busy. I love the feeling of a mini family with each new job you do. I love the traveling involved in my work, and I love researching characters and becoming other people for a job. It's just plain fun and challenging and you meet wonderful people, most of the time. Which leads me to the next question...

Q. Who have you enjoyed working with the most?

A. Obviously the cast of B5 ranks up there with my favorite people in the world. It was a stellar example of like-minded, fun-loving, talented folks coming together and enjoying working with each other. As I mentioned before, Morgan Freeman and Michael Keaton were both sweet to me. The Brat Back guys were fun to work with: Charlie Sheen, Emilio Estevez, Cary Elwes and Nick Cage. I love working with Don Michael Paul, Adam Rifkin and Alan Spencer as directors. Alan Spencer is a very, very funny man, and I hope to work with him again some day. I learned a lot from the old timers like Peter Falk, Burt Lancaster, and Kirk Douglas (I did a tiny role in the film *Tough Guys* with the former two gentlemen. I made it to the cutting room floor I believe!) And I have been amused by Divas of all ages.

Over all I have worked with great people, but there have been some real prima donnas and assholes as well. Actors who don't do "off-camera," flub their lines on purpose, say sexually-explicit things during a scene to screw you up... I had one actor masturbate during a very innocent bed scene. I have had actors show up drunk, on cocaine, late and filthy. I have worked with hung-over actors, angry actors, and competitive, insecure actresses. I have seen an actress throw a cappuccino at a PA because it wasn't "hot enough," and I have seen actors strip their trailers of everything on the last day of the shoot and essentially steal it all from forks to TV's... I have worked with an action star who was told to lose weight and sent to an expensive fat farm only to come out fifty pounds heavier and still ate his way through the movie to the point of not being able to do any stunts or even run! I have worked with misogynists and untalented scumbags but frankly, I don't care. I have had a good time, and I recount the bad stories at every opportunity so that eventually everyone will know what jerks these people are.

Q. What are you up to now?
A. What I always say is, "Five nine, same as always!" Since most actors have websites that keep the fans up to date, this often confuses me as well. If I am at a convention, then THAT is what I am doing at that moment, but to humor people one must make a "list of accomplishments" which for the unemployed actor doing conventions can sometimes be disheartening. Luckily for me I have other interests and jobs such as making music, writing books, directing, making cooking shows and documentaries, stand-up comedy, improv...you name it. Plus I live in two places, London and LA, so there's usually something to talk about. But let me tell you, there's nothing worse than sitting next to someone on an airplane who "sort of" recognizes you, and then you say you're an actress, and then they ask the dreaded, "What have you been in?"

I think from now on I will say to any doctor I meet "Oh, yeah? A doctor? Who are your patients? Nope...don't recognize any of those names!"

As an actress when I am asked this question I end up listing job, after job, after job, and they keep shaking their head and saying... "Nope, never watched that," or they'll say, "I NEVER watch TV or films."

So I'll ask, "Then why do you recognize me?" It's the price of exposure I suppose. I just wish I had the other perks, too, like a full-time masseuse and a personal trainer!

Q. Are you married? Do you have children?
A. No and no.

Q. Why not?
A. Well it's not like I'm turning down dates... people tell me that strong, smart, beautiful women are intimidating... but they never explain MY problem. ☺

The Show Goes On

I never would have thought that a TV series could affect my life so profoundly, but B5 certainly has. I have seen many places I most likely would not have seen if not for B5. I have certainly met thousands of people I never would have met and done things I never would have done if not for the show. In a strange way, doing B5 was even responsible for me moving to England, because I never would have been cast as the lead in a Sci-Fi comedy in the UK if it was not for B5. I did *Star Hyke* in 2005, and ended up loving Britain so much I stayed and still live there half the time today.

I would not have met Holly, Selina, and Michelle Whalen. I would not have done improv all over the world with Dean Haglund and Denise Crosby. I would not have met my dear friend, Nicola Bryant, in London; she befriended me when I hardly knew anyone and needed a friend. I would not have the fun memories of my acquaintances and friendships with Chase Masterson, Paris Jefferson, Mussetta Vander, Armin Shimmerman, Rene Auberjenois and Marina Sirtis. I never would have laughed with Virginia Hey at conventions or counted Linda Thorsen as one of my dear friends. I wouldn't have dated John Flynn for two wonderful years. I would not be having coffee with John Noble and dinner at Bill Mumy's house. I would not have had the pleasure of knowing when Mira Furlan gave birth to her and Goran's beautiful son Marco.

In the end, Babylon 5 gave me a lovely group of people whom I cherish and love, people who are still in my life today. And at the end of the day, when DVD's are obsolete and new shows capture the minds of fans all over the world, what will I really take away from my experience? My memories of good conventions and bad conventions, of crazy fans and nice fans?

No, what I'll really be left with is something far less dramatic yet far more important – a human connection.

I am proud to have been in Babylon 5, and I am proud to have touched so many people in some small way and to have them still recall me with kindness. I thank everyone whom I have ever met at a con, whether I spilled a drink on you or laughed at your bad jokes, we met, we connected, and we will always have that.

People always ask me to tell the story of the end of B5 and why I was not in the last season and all of that stuff... and I was going to take this opportunity to state again my side of the story, but frankly I don't care to tell it again here and now. But know this; if you ever see me and I have a free moment, I will tell you the truth. I promise. That's my little gift to each and every one of you.

I would like to thank Selina Rosen for editing and publishing this book, Holly Evans for getting the fans to send in photos, and for not calling me before 11:00 AM while I was writing. Many thanks to each and every one of you who sent in photos and artwork; this would not have been possible without your pics and permission to use them! A huge thanks to the fans who have supported shows and actors and actresses and creators over the years; without you we would be nothing.

Thanks for making me laugh, cry, travel and explore. Thanks for showing me your hearts and souls and for sharing YOUR stories with me. May we all meet again on this journey called life.

God Bless all of you,
Claudia Christian.

About the Cover Photographer

As a photographer in the motion picture industry, Robert Zuckerman's images have become the cornerstone of advertising and publicity campaigns for such films as *The Crow*, *Bad Boys 2*, *Any Given Sunday*, *Training Day*, *Terminator 3*, and *National Treasure* among others, as well as television series including *The Shield* and *Nip/Tuck*. He photographed the cover for Will Smith's latest CD, "Lost and Found" and did the poster shoot for Will's upcoming film *Pursuit of Happyness*. Zuckerman has recently become the official photographer for the family of Malcolm X.

Robert is one of Claudia's oldest, dearest friends and is her favorite photographer on the planet.

About the Graphic Artist

Gilles Nuytens is a Belgian artist specialized in webdesign. He has worked for several Sci-Fi insiders including Claudia Christian and Denise Crosby. He studied fine arts in Saint Luc in Brussels, one of Europe's most reputed schools. After graduating with a specialization in comic strips, he found a better way to express himself in the webdesign industry. As a big Sci-Fi lover, he has designed several popular Sci-Fi websites.

Gilles has always dreamed of being an actor or a writer. He loves to travel the world and to discover new things. Photography is also one of his favorite hobbies, and he never misses an opportunity to photograph beautiful landscapes during his travels.

Being a romantic, he hopes to someday win enough money to be able to make a world tour with his beloved (who has yet to be determined.) -- Gilles Nuytens www.thescifiworld.net

About the Cover Designer

Why Selina wanted a bio on me I will never know... but here goes. I grew up in San Diego, traveled the world while in the Air Force, and at the end of the first Gulf War they said "sorry we don't need you any more." That led to me to Georgia, where I met Claudia in 1994, and thirteen years later we still work together. I can definitely say she changed my life for the better.

Through this crazy business of conventions I have met all sorts of people who have become my dear friends – like Selina who taught me to sword fight at midnight and Pascale who helped produced Claudia's album "Once Upon a Time" (which is available at CD Baby... shameless plug). Pascale also introduced me to Gilles – an amazing graphic artist who has worked on several projects including this one. I am also very lucky to work with some cool actors and work on a variety of· fun projects... like Dean Haglund from the X-Files who is an amazing improv guy. I got Dean involved with Claudia and Denise Crosby, and they have a very funny show called *Q vs. Janeway* and *Hide and Q*. You can check out Dean's website at www.deanhaglund.com and see the clips... yes, another shameless plug.

Thanks to everyone who buys this book and by all means I hope it makes you laugh – Claudia really is the funniest woman I know. Also a big shout out to Char, Rachel, and Traci who help keep me sane and all the fans out there who have kept me entertained all these years... Holly.

More Shameless Plugs...

Forbidden Love: Wicked Women – Introducing Claudia Christian's debut in writing erotic fiction. Dangerous beauties, seductive sirens, these women know what they want, how they want it and nothing is going to stand in their way. Under the Moon is proud to present a collection of tales that will leave you breathless and wanting more. http://www.genreconnections.com/shop/product.php?productid=16284&cat=259

Chillpak – cool it down/speed it up ww.chillpak.com (invented by Dean Haglund)

Claudia's CD is available at CDBABY.com – just type in Claudia Christian

IMPROV DVD's of Dean and Claudia and Denise are available at Deanhaglund.com

All other autographed memorabilia is available at Claudiachristian.net

Links to other books she has written are on the link page at Claudiachristian.net

Yard Dog Press Titles As Of This Print Date

A Game of Colors
John Urbancik

A Man, A Plan, (yet lacking)
A Canal, Panama
Linda Donahue

Adventures Of the
Irish Ninja
Selina Rosen

All The Marbles
Dusty Rainbolt

Almost Human
Gary Moreau

Ard Magister
Laura J. Underwood

Blackrose Avenue
Mark Shepherd

The Boat Man
Selina Rosen

Bobby's Troll
John Lance

Bogie Woods
Laura J. Underwood

The Bubba Chronicles
Selina Rosen

Bubbas Of the Apocalypse
Edited by Selina Rosen

Chronicles of the Last War
Laura J. Underwood

Dadgum Martians Invade
the Lucky Nickel Saloon
Ken Rand

Dark & Stormy Nights
Bradley H. Sinor

Deja Doo
Edited by Selina Rosen

Diva
Mark W. Tiedemann

Dracula's Lawyer
Julia S. Mandala

The Essence of Stone
Beverly A. Hale

Extensions
Mark Tiedemann

Fire & Ice
Selina Rosen

Flush Fiction, Volume I:
Stories To Be Read In One
Sitting
Edited by Selina Rosen

The Folly of Assumption
Lee Martindale

The Fountain and Other
Stories
Carey G. Osborne

The Four Bubbas of the
Apocalypse: Flatulence,
Halitosis, Incest, and...
Ned
Edited by Selina Rosen

The Four Redheads of the
Apocalypse
Linda L. Donahue, Rhonda
Eudaly, Julia S. Mandala, &
Dusty Rainbolt

The Garden In Bloom
Jeffrey Turner

The Golems
Of Laramie County
Ken Rand

Hammer Town
Selina Rosen

(Continued on the next page)

Texistani: Indo-Pak Food From A Texas Kitchen
Beverly A. Hale

That's All Folks
J. F. Gonzalez

Through Wyoming Eyes
Ken Rand

Tick Hill
Billy Eakin

To Stand As Witness
Lee Martindale

Veil Of the Soul
Trey R.Barker

Wings of Morning
Katharine Eliska Kimbriel

Double Dogs:

#1:
Of Stars & Shadows
Mark W. Tiedemann
This Instance Of Me
Jeffrey Turner

#2:
Gods and Other Children
Bill D. Allen
Tranquility
Tracy Morris

#3:
Home Is the Hunter
James K. Burk
Farstep Station
Lazette Gifford

Non-YDP titles we distribute:

Checking On Culture
Lee Killough

Redgunk Tales
William Eakin

Three Ways to Order:

1. Write us a letter telling us what you want, then send it along with your check or money order (made payable to Yard Dog Press) to: Yard Dog Press, 710 W. Redbud Lane, Alma, AR 72921-7247

2. Use selinarosen@cox.net or lynnstran@cox.net to contact us and place your order. Then send your check or money order to the address above. *This has the advantage of allowing you to check on the availability of short-stock items such as T-shirts and back-issues of Yard Dog Comics.*

3. Contact us as in #1 or #2 above and pay with a credit card or by debit from your checking account. Either give us the credit card information in your letter/Email/phone call, or go to our website and sign up for PayPal. If you send us your information, please include your name as it appears on the card, your credit card number, the expiration date, and for Discover we also need the 4-digit security code after your signature on the back. Please remember that we will include $3.00 S/H for mailing in the lower 48 states.

Watch our website at
www.yarddogpress.com
for news of upcoming projects
and new titles!!

A Note to Our Readers

We at Yard Dog Press understand that many people buy used books because they simply can't afford new ones. That said, and understanding that not everyone is made of money, we'd like you to know something that you may not have realized. Writers only make money on new books that sell. At the big houses a writer's entire future can hinge on the number of books they sell. While this isn't the case at Yard Dog Press, the honest truth is that when you sell or trade your book or let many people read it, the writer and the publishing house aren't making any money.

As much as we'd all like to believe that we can exist on love and sweet potato pie, the truth is we all need money to buy the things essential to our daily lives. Writers and publishers are no different.

We realize that these "freebies" and cheap books often turn people on to new writers and books that they wouldn't otherwise read. However we hope that you will reconsider selling your copy, and that if you trade it or let your friends borrow it, you also pass on the information that if they really like the author's work they should consider buying one of their books at full price sometime so that the writer can afford to continue to write work that entertains you.

We appreciate all our readers and *depend* upon their support.

Thanks,
The Editorial Staff
Yard Dog Press

PS – Please note that "used" books without covers have, in most cases, been stolen. Neither the author nor the publisher has made any money on these books because they were supposed to be pulped for lack of sales.

Please do not purchase books without covers.